BUS BREAKERS OF THE UK

KEITH A. JENKINSON

AMBERLEY

First published 2025

Amberley Publishing
The Hill, Stroud
Gloucestershire, GL5 4EP

www.amberley-books.com

ISBN 978 1 3981 0566 9 (print)
ISBN 978 1 3981 0567 6 (ebook)

British Library Cataloguing in Publication Data.
A catalogue record for this book is available from the British Library.

Origination by Amberley Publishing.
Printed in the UK.

Appointed GPSR EU Representative: Easy Access System Europe Oü, 16879218
Address: Mustamäe tee 50, 10621, Tallinn, Estonia
Contact Details: gpsr.requests@easproject.com, +358 40 500 3575

Introduction

I have been fascinated by bus and coach scrapyards for over seventy years and along the way have become good friends with many of their owners, who have always been happy to chat to me and allow me access into their premises. The manner in which buses are scrapped has changed dramatically over the years. Modern machinery now plays a major role in health and safety, and environmental laws have a massive impact on the procedures. Gone are the days when all that was needed was a muddy field, a sledgehammer and unbelievable energy, and in their place are concreted yards, cranes, mechanical grabs, and safe storage places for batteries, old tyres and drained fluids.

Bus breakers have always been an integral part of the passenger transport industry, first appearing in the 1920s and constantly growing through to the present day. Over the last 100 years there have been more than 150 concerns across the UK who have featured in the dismantling process, some only lasting for a few months while others have survived for several decades. To mention every single one would have filled many more pages than this publication allows. Thus, I have had to concentrate on the larger and better-known companies, and hope that this will not disappoint.

Without the valued help of good friends who share my interest, there would have been many gaps in the photographic content of this book. I would like to particularly thank Jeremy Dickinson, Paul Emery, John Law, Campbell Morrison and John Sinclair, as well as the late Barry Newsome, Trevor Leach and Fred York. Those that are unknown have been credited to my own collection, and to them I am extremely grateful too.

I hope that readers will enjoy this brief history and seeing a selection of photographs, and that the pages that follow will bring back memories of buses and coaches of a bygone era.

Keith A. Jenkinson

A History of Bus Breakers Across the UK

Familiar all over the world in a variety of shapes, sizes and colours, buses and coaches are a part of the daily scene. They take us to school, work, shopping, on holiday and bring us home again, and can be seen everywhere carrying out their daily duties. But what happens to them when they become time expired and are replaced by new, more sophisticated models? This is a question often asked as many people assume that such large vehicles are not easily disposable. The answer is simple: most are dismantled, and the metals from which they are constructed are then able to be recycled for new uses. In the past a few found new lives in non-passenger-carrying roles, such as static caravans or storage units on farms, etc. However, following the introduction of new environmental regulations during the 1950s and early 1960s, these too ultimately followed their compatriots to the breaker's yard and were soon reduced to piles of tangled metal.

Scrappers were established in a wide variety of areas of Britain in the days between the two world wars. A large number were located in Yorkshire, largely due to the close proximity of the steelworks around Rotherham and Sheffield. First, however, to set the scene we must look back to the mid-1920s when the first businesses devoted specifically to the scrapping of buses and other large commercial vehicles were established. One of the initial entrants in this field was Thomas Allsop, who, in 1926, took premises at Worthing Road, Attercliffe, Sheffield. Most of his vehicles were purchased either directly from operators or from J. W. Hall of Huddersfield, who at that time was one of the largest bus and coach dealers in the north of England. Hall took older vehicles in part exchange for more youthful ones, although he was able to resell a large proportion of his stock for further use, those buses and charabancs that were deemed to be time expired were sold on to Allsop. They were then dismantled for numerous resalable parts and the residue dispatched to metal factors in and around Sheffield for recycling. Before many years had elapsed, however, such had been the growth of Allsop's business that its Attercliffe premises were proving to be too small for the number of vehicles awaiting their fate. As a result, a new site was found at Woodsetts Aerodrome near Worksop to where all his activities were transferred in 1933.

Meanwhile, bus dismantling also came to the fore in and around Leeds and Bradford, an area which at that time was largely dominated by the engineering and textile industries. Among the pioneers here was James Stanley Kaye, who, after working for his father Walter in his business in York Road, Leeds, selling used car and motorcycle spares, decided to set up in his own right dismantling cars and a small number of

Ford T buses and selling the spare parts they yielded. To this end he leased a plot of land on St Paul's Street in the heart of Leeds in 1923, but quickly finding this to be of inadequate size, he relocated to a larger site on the fringe of the city at Holme Street, off South Accommodation Road. In the meantime, Mr L. W. Elvins had set up a similar business at Percy Street, Hull, under the title J. W. North, but after finding that this was perhaps geographically unsuited for expansion, he began to seek a more central location, favouring Leeds due to its close proximity to several other large towns. This led him to purchase some land at Whinmoor, some 6 miles from Leeds on the York Road and adjacent to a railway line. As a small stone-built workshop and several tiny outbuildings were already in situ on this site, these provided an amount of undercover storage space for vehicle spares, as well as affording facilities where maintenance could be carried out on vehicles destined for resale. After forming a liaison with J. S. Kaye, it was decided in 1938 to merge the two businesses under the name of W. North. Under this agreement a large area of land was acquired to the south of Leeds at Stourton, where all the buses and coaches bought for resale were amassed. Meanwhile, J. S. Kaye had vacated his Holme Street premises and relocated to Pontefract Road, Stourton, not far from the new W. North site. Here he built a petrol station and car showroom to continue his sales business and although this was completely separate from his involvement in W. North, some bus dismantling was undertaken until the outbreak of the Second World War under the umbrella of another of his companies, Dismantlers and Autowreckers, on a small plot of adjacent land. Then, J. S. Kaye purchased the Whinmoor premises from L. W. Elvins for use in connection with his car business, although in the late 1940s this was closed and used by W. North for the storage of buses awaiting resale or cannibalisation.

Also entering the field of vehicle dismantling during the mid-1930s was P. M. Morrell, who set up in business from rented offices at No. 3 Oxford Place in Leeds city centre before acquiring premises on Hunslet Road, Leeds, where his resale stock was housed and his dismantling activities were undertaken. Morrell's business quickly gained momentum and was later expanded when he entered into an agreement with the previously mentioned Thomas Allsop, a collaboration that continued until the outbreak of the Second World War, after which he continued in business independently until 1955. Although few of the buses purchased by Morrell found new operational homes, a large number were sold for use as static caravans or holiday homes, a common sight in numerous parts of Britain until new rural planning regulations caused their demise in the late 1950s.

Bus breaking in the 1920s and 1930s was a physically demanding occupation, with little mechanised equipment being available to assist those employed in this work. The dismantling of a bus or coach was a slow, laborious task in those far off days, with nuts, bolts and screws all having to be removed by hand, mechanical components taken out with only the most basic of equipment, and what remained of the vehicle having to be destroyed by the wielding of a sledgehammer or by setting fire to it. With few regulations relating to environmental or health and safety issues, there were not many restrictions governing the process of vehicle dismantling; thus, whatever means were easiest were used.

Following the outbreak of the Second World War, new regulations imposed by the Ministry of Supply dictated that life expired and surplus vehicles of all types should be placed in store rather than be sold or dismantled and that all scrap metals should be redirected to the 'war effort'. This led to several of the established bus and coach dismantlers leaving the industry, at least for the duration of the hostilities. While some recommenced their activities after peace returned in 1945, several instead turned their attention towards the buying and selling of war surplus goods and materials and never restarted vehicle dismantling.

Thus, it was not until the late 1940s that the wholesale scrapping of buses and coaches began to regain its momentum, with most operators having had little choice but to 'make do and mend' and continue operating their pre-war stock until new replacement vehicles became available. During this period several new bus breakers began to enter the fray, particularly in the London area where a large number of former London buses ended their days. In October 1948, Cox & Danks Ltd, who dated back to 1913 when it was set up in Oldbury in the West Midlands in 1913 as a maritime salvage company, gained a contract from London Transport (who had previously scrapped its buses at its Chiswick works) to scrap the bodies of its time-expired vehicles and return their chassis to Chiswick, where they were dismantled for spares. To undertake this task, Cox & Danks leased a plot of wasteland on Faggs Road at Feltham, Middlesex, where it dealt with over 670 ST, LT and STLs before ceasing its operation in June 1949. Meanwhile, two months earlier in April, London Transport issued a similar contract to R. L. Daniels Ltd of Britannia Metal Works, London, E14, who took on the lease of a 10-acre site at Ferry Lane, Rainham, Essex, where this work would be carried out. On this occasion, however, Daniels scrapped the whole bus after London Transport staff working on-site had removed selected mechanical units, driving mirrors and tyres, etc., for returning to Chiswick.

During the next two years, around 2,000 London buses met their fate at Rainham, with only a tiny handful escaping to enjoy further leases of live with travelling showmen or as caravans. Following this, in May 1951 London Transport issued another contract to scrap a small number of its buses, all of its trams and a number of its trolleybuses. On this occasion the contract was given to George Cohen & Sons Ltd, whose history dates back to 1834 when it was based in London's East End and, like Cox & Danks, was also heavily involved in maritime salvage. Initially Cohen did his breaking on a plot of land used by London Transport on Penhall Road, Charlton, close to its tram/trolleybus workshops, where all the trams suffered their fate along with fifty London Transport wartime Guy Arabs, around 120 AEC Regent STLs, and from 1959 a few trolleybuses too. After departing from this site at the end of the decade, Cohen began scrapping London's trolleybuses on a plot of land alongside the undertaking's Colindale depot. Later, in the 1960s, it also dismantled a small number of buses at its Canning Town and Kettering premises.

Although the above were the main bus breakers in the London area, a few other companies came and went, such as Max Speed Transportation at Mitcham (1952–60), George Groves at Merton Abbey (*c.* 1956–62) and C. F. Hill, who traded as Clapham Commercials at Battersea (1963–78). Slightly further afield, Lansdowne/AMCC had yards at Frating and Southend in the 1950s, while much later Erith Commercials began its activities at Belvedere, near Dartford, in 2004 and still continues today. Originally concentrating on Mercedes-Benz minibuses, in 2007 it expanded by breaking larger buses and coaches (mainly at its other yard at Bean) and became a major seller of engines and other mechanical units to overseas customers, the majority of which were in African countries.

While bus breaking was never a major industry south of London, it nevertheless took place in a few places along the south coast and in Devon. Located in two yards at Hedge End, near Southampton, was T. Jefferies, who began his activities in 1935 and continued until 1975, during which time he also traded as Docks Haulage Co. at Botley. Meanwhile, in 1950 J. Light of Southerham, near Lewes, began bus scrapping but ceased after just two years before starting again in 1958 and continuing until around 1970, albeit only in a small way, while Jordan scrapped buses on a site near Portsmouth gasworks at Hilsea. Other breakers in this area – such as Strudwick at Horndean and later at Bedhampton, and Cooper at Ringmer – came and went in the 1950s and 1960s. Also joining the fray in 1955 were C. Morgan at Waltham Chase, who continued for a number of years, and Cranes & Commercials at Bishops Waltham, who was active from 1972 to 1985. Then, 9 miles to the east was Fort Wallington, which was one of the notorious 'Palmerston Follies' built in the 1860s and designed to protect Portsmouth harbour from enemy attack. After use by the Royal Navy, it was eventually demilitarised and subject to demolition, but after its structural strength made this too difficult the process was abandoned and instead it was used for commercial purposes. One of its new occupants was A. Mills. who in 1965 set up in business as Wallingford Commercials and began scrapping all types of vehicles, among which were around 200 buses, many of which had been acquired from T. Jefferies and C. Morgan. In 1971 Mills moved elsewhere for business, albeit only dismantling cars and light commercials. Along the coast in the opposite direction was Rundle at Laira Bridge, Plymouth, Devon, who entered the industry in 1958 and continued until 1974; Pearce, also in Plymouth; and J. Orchard & Son, who despite being largely a car breaker dabbled in bus breaking at St Day, Cornwall, for around ten years from 1977.

Moving northwards from London, there were several bus breakers in East Anglia, albeit most of them only being small concerns. Among the better known is D. J. Spall Recycling Ltd at Dallinghoo, north-east of Ipswich, who began mainly as a car breaker in 1971. It was not until the mid-1990s that they ventured into bus dismantling, albeit in a small way, but they still remain in business today. Much further north, in Norfolk, Ben Jordan entered the field of bus breakers at Coltishall, on the outskirts of Norwich, in 1949, initially buying most of his stock from Eastern Counties Omnibus Co. Originally working from a small yard adjacent to his residence, this was quickly found to be too small for his growing business, which led him to rent a wooded area behind a farm a few miles away at Horstead, and several years later on the site of a disused military airfield. An eccentric man, rather than dismantle his ever-increasing stock, he instead stored it while waiting for the price of scrap metal to rise. It rose and fell numerous times over an approximately thirty-year period before any serious dismantling took place. Now faced with a mammoth task, in 1984/85 he sold a number of buses to South Yorkshire breaker Geoff Ripley, who towed them over 160 miles to his premises for their ultimate destruction. Then after falling foul of new environmental regulations, Jordan eventually cleared his yards before his death in May 2002. What remained of his business passed to his son, who diversified into scrapping cars.

Across country are two more recent bus breakers: MC Tractors and Shelton Motors, both of whom are located not far from each other in Ramsey, near Huntingdon, and have connections with each other. MC Tractors began trading on April 2008 and were basically dismantlers, while Shelton Motors was established in 1950 and for many years concentrated on lorry and plant sales before diversifying into bus breaking around ten years ago. As well as purchasing buses for dismantling from numerous different operators, a large number of their acquisitions came from Ensign (dealer) at Purfleet. Another bus breaker near Huntingdon was Joe Hunt at Molesworth, who began in 1946 with the purchase of former military vehicles, some of which were sold on for further use while others were scrapped. Later, in the 1960s, he also began buying time-expired buses, and scrapped a number at a quarry he owned at Burton Magna while a few languished at his main premises until he retired in 1997.

Moving west into Wales, one of the main bus dismantlers was W. A. Way, who set up in business in 1946 on a plot of land leased at East Cardiff Dock. After working several years on his own, in 1960 he entered into a partnership with a Mr Woodfield, although this proved to be short-lived and in 1961 he reverted to operating independently. Most of his purchases came from Welsh municipal and independent bus and coach operators, and included were a number of Cardiff trolleybuses. Later, in 1981 he took another partner, Mr Williams. The business was renamed Way & Williams Ltd and relocated to Treforrest in 1982, then three years later to Tonteg before retiring soon afterwards. Prior to leaving Cardiff, while he was away on holiday his son (allegedly without his father's knowledge) sold a sizeable number of his buses to Trevor Wigley at Carlton (South Yorkshire) where they ultimately met their fate.

Way was not the only bus breaker in South Wales, however, as in 1945 G. H. Morgan set up as a dealer and breaker at Pengam, and nine years later formed an association with Newport-based South Wales Motor Traders, a company that had been selling used buses and coaches since 1933. It would appear that both companies ceased trading in the late 1950s, leaving the field open for Way and a small number of new short-lived breakers who never grew in size. One who did survive for a longer period, however, was Jones, who began operating at Cardiff Docks in the 1950s and continued until 1965 before relocating to Pontllanfraith where he continued for a few more years.

In more recent times, some newcomers have entered the industry in South Wales. One example is Abba Scrap Metals at Dowlais on the fringe of Merthyr Tydfil, who started in business in 2006 as car dismantlers but quickly added buses and coaches to its portfolio. Prior to this, another company known as JAB93 began scrapping cars and light commercial vehicles at Bridgend in 1993, and since the mid-2010s they've also turned their attention to buses and coaches. Also joining the fray was Ammanford Metal Recyclers, who started life as a car dealer in 2011 and later diversified into vehicle dismantling, which included buses and coaches. All three of these companies are still active today.

Back in England, in 1953 Marton (Warwickshire) coach operator Harry Aston and PSV dealer Henry Bowen (who had previously been with dealer Frank Cowley at Salford) formed a partnership to sell buses and coaches under the title PVD (Marton), but this proved to be short-lived. After amicably parting company in 1954, Bowen went on to form Passenger Vehicles Disposals and Fleet Car Sales at Dunchurch, both of which were primarily concerned with sales rather than dismantling. Although a few vehicles were scrapped there, most of the buses deemed to be unsalable for further use were disposed of to Colbro Ltd (who also traded as Diesel Engine Exporters), which was started in 1955 by George Corson at Rothwell near Leeds – there will be more on this later.

Of greater importance in the Midlands was W. T. Bird & Sons, who entered the scrap business in 1933 at a site on Shipston Road, Stratford-upon-Avon. They later moved to larger premises on Birmingham Road in the same town, becoming one of Britain's largest dealers and breakers. Adjacent to the yard and workshops was a quarry in which a sizeable number of buses were dumped after having their mechanical units and some panels, etc., removed. In 1970 Bird's vacated its Stratford premises and relocated to Long Marston, near Rugby, where it diversified into the scrapping of railway rolling stock and gradually ceased its bus-breaking activities.

Also set up in the West Midlands in 1933 was Holland Brothers at Oldbury, who were second-hand bus and coach dealers as well as dismantlers until the end of the decade, and Cashmores Metals at Great Bridge on the outskirts of Dudley, who also scrapped railway locomotives and rolling stock. After the war several new breakers appeared in the West Midlands, including Devey at Shenstone, near Tamworth; Longbridge Engineering at Brierley Hill; and Brickley at Walsall. However, all of these had disappeared by the mid- to late 1960s.

In 1979 bus and coach operator Martin Perry also began scrapping buses and coaches under the name UK Bus Dismantlers at Bromyard, Herefordshire, which continues today. Then at Hixon in Staffordshire, Jonathan Lloyd Commercial Salvage entered the field in 1998, scrapping all forms of commercial vehicles, including PSVs, many of which were the subject of insurance claims.

In Derbyshire a much older vehicle dismantler was active: Albert Looms, who began his business at Spondon, on the outskirts of Derby, in 1920. Although largely concerned with cars and light commercial vehicles, over the years a number of buses have been dealt with on the company's 7-acre site, particularly examples from the nearby Wellglade Group's Notts & Derby subsidiary. However, due to ill health it was decided in June 2024 to close the business, which was still family owned, and clear the site over the next couple of months.

Moving northwards, after the end of the Second World War Lancashire, particularly an area around Manchester, became a mecca for bus dealers and dismantlers. Among the first to appear was Woodfield & Turner, who traded as Used Units at Whittlefield

Street, Burnley, and began selling and dismantling buses and coaches in 1946. Although it continued in business until 1955, in its latter years it concentrated largely on the retrieval of mechanical units from lorries and vans. Three years later Allied Aluminium Products set up at Dukinfield, where it scrapped a number of buses. Then in 1950 it was joined by travelling showmen S. & J. R. Cubbins, who, during the winter months when travelling fairgrounds were usually at rest, began dismantling buses at Farnworth, near Bolton. Operating from two yards, they continued in business until the late 1960s. Following these breakers, in 1953 D. A. Salmon began his activities at Gorton and moved to Ashbury's Station during the following year, while in 1956 he entered into a partnership with Ron Blair (who had started in 1936) and relocated to Cheetham Hill Road, Manchester, where he remained until the alliance ceased in 1958, after which he started up again as a sole dismantler from premises at Shaw, near Oldham. Never settling anywhere for long, in 1965 he moved yet again, this time to Audenshaw where he began trading under the name of Audenshaw Diesels before leaving the industry completely in 1973. Meanwhile, the aforementioned Ron Blair continued business at new premises in Pendleton before relocating to Princes Bridge, Salford, where he stayed until retiring in 1963. Another newcomer was Shawe, who entered the field in 1957 on a site at Manchester Docks. In that same year C. Coppock set up in business in Elm Grove, Sale, mainly as a second-hand bus and coach dealer but he also stripped time-expired vehicles in order to provide spare parts to those to whom he had sold vehicles before selling them on to Shawe for their final destruction. More recently, in 1982 Blakeleys Recycling Ltd, who started in business as P. T. S. Skip Hire at Platt Bridge near Wigan, expanded into bus breaking (albeit in a small way) in the early 2000s and continued thus until 2018 when the company suddenly closed and surprisingly left a number of partly scrapped vehicles on its site until 2022.

Across the Pennines in Yorkshire bus breaking became a major industry, with numerous companies suddenly springing up since the early 1950s, forty-five of which were located in the Barnsley area. In the meantime, slightly further south was Frederick Booth, who had started life as a general scrap dealer at Armer Street, Rotherham, in 1920 and many years later grew to become a major ferrous and non-ferrous metal recycler in the town, largely scrapping railway locomotives and rolling stock. It was not until the early 1970s that the company began dismantling buses at its Clarence Metal Works, and later in the decade at Aston where it had acquired a site on Ulley Lane. Purchasing large numbers of buses from NBC subsidiaries, municipal undertakings and London Transport, it scrapped several hundred vehicles before giving greater concentration to the other aspects of its business in the mid-1980s. To the east of Rotherham there was Doncaster, where a number of scrap metal businesses began including buses in their activities, one being Barry Jameson, who began in 1973 at a muddy field at Dunscroft. After adopting the name Dunscroft Commercials in 1976, he temporarily left the industry in 1979 and rented his premises to E. Beckett, who moved from Boulder Bridge Lane, Carlton, but returned there in July of the following year. Upon his departure, Jameson set up again dismantling buses, this time under the name Doncaster Bus Breakers, although from the mid-1980s rather than completing the scrapping process he largely stripped out all the mechanical units and then sold the remains to some of the Carlton breakers, mainly PVS.

Among the first of the breakers geographically closer to Barnsley was Alan Finlay, who initially leased a plot of land at Blacker Hill Sidings in 1956. After his business started to grow he moved to premises at Birdwell in 1966, where he began trading as Hartwood Finance, selling buses for further use as well as dismantling them. In around 1970, after gaining a second yard at Worsborough Dale, instead of breaking buses himself he sold the majority of them to Paul Sykes, expanding his empire by selling engines and mechanical units across the globe. Entering the dismantling industry a few years later was Beckett at Pontefract and Dennis Higgs. From 1959 Higgs undertook his activities at Monk Bretton, remaining there until 1977 when he temporarily left and leased his yard to newcomers Dickinson & Shippey. They continued until December 1978 when they too left and the lease was taken up by Geoff Ripley, who stayed there until July 1982 when he moved to a site on Boulder Bridge Lane, Carlton. Surprisingly, Dennis Higgs then recommenced his activities at Monk Bretton and continued until 1984 when he diversified into plant hire.

Moving into the 1960s, Swift began breaking buses at Stairfoot in 1964. Paul Sykes started at Blacker Hill Sidings in 1961 and later passed this to his cousin, Joe Sykes. Arthur Barraclough set up at Shaw Lane, Carlton. Brian Laverack, Arnold Pickersgill (who later traded as PVS), Benny Johnson and James Whiting all entered the industry at South Elmsall. Trevor Wigley and Frank Wells began at Goldthorpe in 1975, and Ronald Askin obtained premises alongside Yorkshire Traction's depot on Upper Sheffield Road, Barnsley, towards the end of the decade. With bus breakers not being welcomed by the residents of South Elmsall, all those carrying out their activities there quickly began to seek new sites. In the late 1960s one was found at Boulder Bridge Lane, Carlton, a muddy and badly drained narrow plot of land with a railway embankment on one side and a National Coal Board coking plant at the other. After the latter's demolition, the land on which it stood was used by the council as a landfill site and has now been transformed into a nature reserve. Most, although not all, of the bus breakers swiftly moved there while Benny Johnson, a nomad who regularly moved from one place to another, found a number of short-term homes at or near Goldthorpe before joining the others at Carlton. After dissolving his short-lived partnership with Frank Wells, Trevor Wigley worked for a while for his relative Brian Laverack at PVS before setting up in his own right in Boulder Bridge Lane in 1977.

During the 1970s and 1980s, PVS became the main scrapper of buses cannibalised by NBC's disposal unit – APT – at Lincoln, as well as all the buses stripped for spares by Purfleet dealer Ensign, although after falling out with the latter in 2005 it was not until Ensign was purchased by First Group in 2023 that the relationship resumed. In the meantime PVS, together with Wigleys, purchased the remaining stock of Wombwell Diesels through an auction in 1994. They also acquired all the vehicles at North East Bus Breakers upon its closure in 1995, all the buses and machinery left in W. North's Sherburn-in-Elmet yard following the company's closure in January 1996 and, similarly, upon Whiting Bros retirement in April 1999 the ninety-six buses that remained at their Ferrybridge site to where they had relocated in the late

1980s. Then, following the death of PVS's owner, Brian Laverack, in December 2019, the business passed to his son Geoffrey, daughter Janice and her husband Phillip. In September 2020 Geoffrey decided to retire and sold his share to his sister and her husband, leaving them now as the sole owners. Prior to all this, in the mid-1970s George Jones dissolved his partnership with Eddie Hardwick and set up in business on his own under the name of Carlton Metals on a plot of land in Shaw Lane, across the road from Boulder Bridge Lane, where he remained until he ceased trading in the late 1980s.

Looking back, for a variety of reasons departures from Boulder Bridge had begun to occur in the 1970s. Benny Johnson left late in that year due to ill health; Whiting Bros and Paul Sykes later in the decade, relocating to Featherstone and Wakefield Road, Barnsley, respectively, after Sykes diversified into second-hand bus and coach sales; and Rollinson exited the industry in 1993, followed by Joe Sykes upon his retirement in 1996. Then, after new health and safety and environmental laws were introduced in the late 1990s the exodus escalated, with some of the breakers finding it too expensive to upgrade their premises and a few others firmly refusing to do so. By 2023 only Hardwick, Parton, PVS, Ripley, Wigley and Beckett remained on Boulder Bridge Lane, all of whom had complied with the new regulations, providing a totally different scene to that witnessed four decades earlier at this location.

Meanwhile, at Wombwell, 5 miles east of Carlton, in 1947, Chris Hoyle had started a business collecting scrap metal with a horse and cart, and as this grew he purchased a second-hand lorry and began to further develop. In 1957, his two sons Chris and Wilf took over the business, and two years later they took the lease on a disused brickworks and began dismantling a few buses. After renaming the business Wombwell Diesels in 1965, it expanded rapidly. A few years later a contract was gained from London Transport to scrap forty RT-type AEC Regent IIIs, leading to a larger contract being negotiated which ultimately resulted in around 4,000 of the capital's redundant RTs, RTLs, RFs, AEC Swifts and Merlins suffering their destruction here. In addition, numerous other buses were purchased from NBC companies, PTEs and municipal undertakings and continued until 1994 when the two brothers retired and ceased their activities, auctioning the few buses still on-site, most of which were purchased by PVS and Wigley at Carlton.

Further north, in West Yorkshire, a few other bus breakers sprung up, most of which were short-lived, however, with only a handful ever achieving growth. While major second-hand bus and coach dealer W. North dismantled a number of buses at its Stourton site in the 1950s and later at Sherburn-in-Elmet (to where it had moved in 1961) to provide spares to customers who had purchased from them, in 1984 it also dismantled fifty Routemasters whose mechanical units had to be returned to London. In addition, after the death in 1952 of Leeds independent bus and coach operator Samuel Ledgard, his friend G. W. Butler, who had started as a general scrap merchant in 1933, purchased all the buses that had unbelievably been stored by Ledgard on the roof of his Armley depot since the 1920s (including some steam wagons) and scrapped them at his Bowling Iron Works and Menston yards. These were the only buses dealt with by Butler, who then reverted to his established activities. Meanwhile, in the 1950s brothers Bob and Tony Lockey set up as dealers and breakers of former military vehicles at a small yard high up on the moors between Bradford and Keighley, but in 1960 also turned their attention to dismantling buses and trolleybuses, largely from local municipal undertakings. After reforming their business as Bingley Autospares in 1963, they acquired a quarry adjacent to their small maintenance building and it was there that, similar to Bird's at Stratford-upon-Avon, most of their acquired vehicles met their end after having many of their mechanical units removed for resale. After adding passenger-carrying vehicles from Lancashire and North East municipal operators, by the mid-1990s they ceased these activities and diversified into scrapping cars and light commercials after filling in the quarry with its remains still buried beneath.

Across in the Leeds area, in 1955 previously mentioned Colbro Ltd/Diesel Engine Exporters had set up in business at Jaw Bone Works, Rothwell, between Leeds and Wakefield – only around a mile away from W. North's large yard at Stourton. They began dismantling buses that had largely been acquired from PVD/Fleet Car Sales at Dunchurch, while in addition to these a significant number of Newcastle-upon-Tyne, Nottingham and Bournemouth Corporation trolleybuses were acquired and scrapped for their electrical components. These were then were exported to numerous overseas operators, as were a number of combustion-engine buses and coaches that were dismantled for their engines and mechanical units. In the late 1960s, however, the company ceased trading. Another breaker to spring up not far from Colbro in 1956 was Bolland, who initially scrapped lorries in his muddy yard at Wakefield but quickly turned his attention to buses, most of which were acquired from dealer W. North at Stourton. Never expanding, he ended his activities in the early to mid-1960s.

Meanwhile, across in Bradford was Norman Blamires, who started as a car and small commercial vehicle breaker in the mid-1930s on a small strip of land at St Dunstans, close to the city centre. Early in the 1950s, however, he turned his attention to buses and coaches, some of which he acquired directly from their operators and others from dealers such as W. North. Joined by his stepson Brian Jackson in 1964, he continued to grow his business on his small, cramped site until his death in December 1965, after which Jackson took over. He continued until 1970 when he vacated the site and left the industry. There were a few other bus breakers who tried their luck around the area, but those who did only managed to last for short periods of time. One of these was Danny Parker, who had worked as a delivery/collection driver for W. North and then took the decision to start up in his own right as a bus breaker alongside a disused textile mill near the centre of Bradford. Unfortunately, this was not successful and within a year he had returned to his previous job at W. North.

There were several bus breakers of different sizes in County Durham and Northumberland, some of whom survived for numerous years while others came and went in shorter periods of time. Among the oldest established were Basey, a travelling showman at Langley Moor who from 1935 dismantled buses in the winter months of each year until the mid-1960s; Tremble at Benton, Newcastle-upon-Tyne; Veti at Sunderland; and Thompson at Darlington – all from the late 1930s. There was also

W. H. Arnott Young, who started as a maritime breaker near Glasgow around 1920. Later expanding as a general metal recycler, it opened branches in several places around the UK, one of which was at Dinsdale, Darlington, where it began breaking buses, mainly from United Automobile Services in 1950 and then at Middleton St George in 1965. Joining the industry after the Second World War were several smaller breakers, including Monte, Fencehouses, in 1965, Morley at Shildon from 1967 to 1972, R. Beck at Burnopfield from 1971 to 1979 and Blackett, Butterknowle, who was already established as a car breaker before adding bus breaking to its portfolio in the late 1960s and continuing thus until 1986 when it returned to its roots. Following these came North East Bus Breakers, who set up as bus and coach dealers at Craghead and later diversified into breaking at a new site at Annfield Plain in 1991, where it remained until it ceased trading in 2002.

Across the River Tyne in Northumberland was Houghton, who traded as Transport Spares Ltd at Blyth in the mid-1950s. They relocated to Bedlington in 1958 and remained there for around ten years until ceasing trading. Another breaker to end its activities there (in 1974) was Hancock & Turner, who had begun at Lynemouth in 1962 and had moved to Bedlington Station in 1972. Also active between 1977 and 1981 was Willoughby at Ashington, but none of these could be classed as large companies and all had concentrated on small numbers of buses acquired from local independent operators. Moving forward into more recent times, Alpha Recovery at Weetslade started as a vehicle recovery company in 1987 specialising in rescuing lorries and heavy haulage vehicles. In the early 2000s, in addition to this they began purchasing buses and coaches for scrapping and quickly expanded in this field to become a major player still active today.

Over the border in Scotland, bus breaking was undertaken at several locations across the country, some concerns having been established in the 1920s while others are relative newcomers. Looking back to 1923, Sanderson set up in business at Glasgow as a bus and coach dealer and then relaunched in 1932 as Millburn Motors before later opening a branch at Walmer Bridge in Lancashire. In addition to dealing he also undertook some dismantling to provide spares to those who had purchased vehicles from him. Meanwhile, in 1929 a new dealer/breaker named Locke appeared on the scene in Edinburgh, where he remained until the early 1980s. In 1932 yet another dismantler – Finlay – began his activities in Falkirk and continued until 1967. Shortly before the start of the Second World War, Chalmers began scrapping buses at Leith where yet another breaker, Hunter, entered the scene in 1946 at Seafield. Following the untimely death of his father, his son Bernard took over the business and after a few years relocated to Gilmerton, where he remained active until 1990 after having diversified into heavy plant hire. Two years after Hunter's appearance, Salsburgh bus and coach operator Irvine, who traded as Tiger Coaches, added dealing and scrapping to their portfolio and continued with both until the early 1990s when they returned to coach operation. Next to take up the challenge of bus recycling was Lundie at Riccarton, Kilmarnock, conveniently not very far from Western SMT's headquarters, who continued in business until 1958 before leaving to pursue other interests. Similarly, close to Scottish Omnibuses' head office in Kirkcaldy, another breaker to set up in business in 1961 was Muir, who remained in the business until 1986. Much further north, in 1967 Kelbie began dismantling buses at Turriff in Aberdeenshire, where they remained active until the late 1980s. In the meantime, however, a breaker who expanded to ultimately become Scotland's largest bus breaker was R. W. Dunsmore, who started his activities in the early 1960s at Larkhall, some 14 miles south-east of Glasgow. After being passed to his son Jack and growing considerably, the company ultimately found its yard to be too small and began storing buses awaiting scrapping at a number of local bus operators' premises, including McKindless at Wishaw and in a quarry at West Calder alongside Prentice Westwood's depot. In 1986, in addition to its dismantling activities, Dunsmore's began a commercial vehicle recovery business. Five years later they moved to a larger yard at Strutherhill Industrial Estate at Larkhall where they remained until the owner's untimely death in January 2005. The business was continued by his family until it eventually closed in 2019. Meanwhile, in 2005, another recovery company – M8 at Rutherglen – took the opportunity to start bus breaking under the name of 'End of Life Vehicles'. Also entering the scene were dealer Campbell at Alexandria, who is still in business today, and Clyde Metals Recycling at Greenock, who has been in business for around fifty years but had only added buses to its portfolio in the 2020s.

Across the Irish Sea, bus breaking on the Isle of Man was comparatively rare, with most redundant buses finding new uses as farm sheds or racetrack grandstands, etc. However, established general scrap merchants Manx Metals at Ballasalla dismantled a small number of Douglas Corporation buses in the 1960s and 1970s before a new entrant to the field – Motor Salvage – started in 1983 in a quarry at Point of Ayre on the northern tip of the island. Although a sizeable number of buses were scrapped there in 1984/85, the company then concentrated on cars and light commercials until ceasing trading in 1999 after Isle of Man Transport began selling its buses to the UK mainland for continued service.

Further across the water, Ulster hosted a number of bus breakers, several of which had suddenly sprung up as a result of the Troubles in the 1980s/90s. The largest of these was G. W. J. Beattie, who had set up in business at Hillsborough in 1967 and had been responsible for the demise of a large number of Belfast Corporation's trolleybuses and motorbuses. As the Troubles grew, so did Beattie's business, despite some smaller concerns such as Miller at Castlereagh, J. Corry at Campsie (near Londonderry) and G. O'Neill (who also traded as GO Skips) at Belfast disposing of the remains of buses destroyed by terrorist attacks. Shortly after the new millennium, however, Beattie gradually diversified into heavy plant and crane hire and ultimately ceased scrapping buses in 2004, leaving Hamill & Sons at Ahoghill in County Antrim to fill the gap in 2004 and become Ulster's main bus disposal company.

As has been shown throughout this chapter, bus breaking has been more prevalent in some parts of the UK than others. It has, however, been undertaken across the entirety of the UK, albeit on a smaller scale in some places. For a wide variety of reasons, including health and safety and environmental issues, the number of older established breakers has gradually diminished over the past three decades, while others have sprung up to fill the gaps on a smaller scale. As said at the start of this potted history, over the years the method of dismantling buses has changed considerably. Sophisticated machinery has replaced the traditional sledgehammer, and new regulations have been attached to the methods of disposing of all the waste materials. Just starting to show signs of further changes needed across the scrap industry are the methods required to safely accommodate gas, hydrogen, and the batteries of electric-powered buses and coaches, all of which will initially prove a challenge to the industry and possibly even further reduce the number of dismantlers, particularly the smaller ones. There are interesting times ahead, one thinks.

Finally, enthusiasts are to be warned that due to health and safety regulations, and sadly the theft of 'souvenirs' from vehicles, entry to any of the premises/yards listed above is not be permitted, and as most are covered by multiple CCTV cameras, you will be seen.

Awaiting its destruction in the yard of breaker Bollands at Wakefield in November 1961 is ex-London Transport central area AEC Q-type CLE 133, which had stood in the Stourton premises of dealer W. North since the year after its withdrawal from service in 1953. (K. A. Jenkinson)

In the first stage of scrapping at W. North's, Sherburn-in-Elmet, in 1984 are two unidentified ex-London Routemasters, with others awaiting their fate behind the wall in the background. (Jeremy Dickinson)

Seen in 1996 being scrapped by Wigley (breaker), Carlton, in W. North's (dealer) Sherburn-in-Elmet yard where it had stood since 1987, is ex-West Yorkshire Road Car Co. Duple Dominant-bodied Leyland Leopard UWR 769R, which started life in July 1977. (Jeremy Dickinson)

Lined up awaiting their fate in Daniels', Rainham's yard in early 1950 are five ex-London Transport double-deck LT-type AEC Renowns, two STLs and a pair of single-deck AECs – either LTs or Ts. Nearest the camera on the right are LT class GK 2072 and STL EGO 360. (Author's collection)

Nearing its end in April 1951, London Transport-rebuilt E1 1398 (complete except for some missing windows) stands in the Penhall Road Charlton yard, in which George Cohen scrapped numerous LT trams and buses. (David Bailey collection)

Huddled together behind London Transport's Colindale depot are a number of 1936 vintage Birmingham & Wagon Co.-bodied Leyland TTB2 B1 class trolleybuses, including 86 and 73. All were awaiting dismantlement in 1960 on this site by George Cohen. (Author's collection)

Seen here being scrapped by George Cohen at its Canning Town site in April 1964 is London Transport pre-war RT118, which was new in 1941. Peeping in on the left is an ex-London post-war RT. (Author's collection)

Pictured being dismantled in one of London bus dealer/breaker AMCC's yards is this Roe-bodied AEC Regent I, which had begun life with Leeds Corporation in 1934. (Neil Halliday collection)

Awaiting its fate as it stands in front of a fire escape ladder unit on a plot of land in Hilsea on 14 March 1963 is a former Portsmouth Corporation trolleybus – still with its booms on its roof. (David Bradley)

Neatly parked on the premises of local bus breaker Pearce *c.* 1980 are sixteen ex-Plymouth City Transport Leyland Atlanteans whose operational days have sadly come to an end. (Ken Baker)

With the remains of Fort Wallington in the background, two SMT-bodied Bedford OWBs that had served with Devizes-based contractors Chivers await their destruction at Wallington Commercials in November 1967. (R. E. Gray)

Reclining by some of the remains of the old fort at Wallington Commercials' yard in February 1967 while it awaits its fate is former Atomic Power Constructions, Dungeness, ECW-bodied Bristol K6A FFM 450, which had started life with Crosville in May 1946. (F. W. York)

Awaiting scrapping at Fort Wallington in 1968 are ex-Gosport & Fareham's ex-Halifax Corporation Park Royal-bodied AEC Regent 1 (JX 7048), an ex-Glasgow AEC Regent and former Northern General NCB-bodied AEC Regent II ACN 172. (F. W. York)

Standing alongside an ex-Aldershot & District East Lancs-bodied Dennis Lance in the yard of Jeffries, Hedge End, in December 1967 is an unidentified all-Leyland lowbridge Titan PD2, which had been new to Ribble Motor Services. (F. W. York)

Seen in the small yard of Barham (breaker), Matching Green, on 25 February 2017 is ex-First Eastern Counties Plaxton-bodied Volvo B10M N615 APU, which had started life with Thamesway in January 1996. (John Podgorski)

Nearing the end of their lives in the Bean yard of Erith Commercials in May 2007 are First Western National Leyland Lynx 62671 (K11 BMS), First Eastern Counties ECW-bodied Leyland Olympian 34359 (KGG 159Y), and First PMT Optare Delta-bodied DAF SB220 60046 (H804 GRE). (D. W. Rhodes)

Squeezed into the small Coltishall yard of Ben Jordan in 1981, where they had rested for several years, are four of ex-Eastern Counties post-war ECW-rebodied Leyland TD2s. (Eric Dean collection)

Rotting at one of Ben Jordan's yards is this coach-bodied Dennis Lancet J3, which had ended its life with Ford & Carter, a contractor in Ipswich. (Eric Dean collection)

Standing on the disused Coltishall airfield, which was used as one of the sites for breaker Ben Jordan, are several ex-Eastern Counties Bristol LSs and VRTs, together with former Maidstone & District Harrington-bodied AEC Reliance TKM 327. (Author's collection)

With all its mechanical units removed and standing upside down at Ben Jordan's airfield site in May 1977 is ECW-bodied Bristol LL5G KNG 715, which was new to Eastern Counties in September 1950 but had latterly served with a contractor. (T. M. Leach collection)

A trio of ex-Eastern Counties ECW-bodied Bristol buses – 1949 highbridge K5G HPW 97, 1964 MW5G AAH 102B and 1948 L5G GPW 697 – await their demise at Ben Jordan's Coltishall airport site in May 1977. (T. M. Leach collection)

Seen in 1996 in breaker Joe Hunt's shed at Molesworth is what is left of an unidentified single-decker last used by contractors Gleeson. (Author's collection)

Pictured at Joe Hunt's premises with its upper deck partly scrapped is ex-Northampton Corporation Roe-bodied Crossley DD42/3 VV 9141. Surprisingly, soon afterwards this was sold for preservation to provide spares for sister VV 9146, which was at that time being restored. (Author's collection)

Pictured being scrapped at Shelton Motors, Ramsey, in early 2024 is ex-Brighton & Hove Mercedes Citaro 0530G bendibus 105 (BD57 WDC), which began life with Go-Ahead London General in February 2008. (Author's collection/Mark Kirk)

Way's yard at Cardiff Docks in January 1973 shows a variety of vehicles awaiting their fate, including a couple of ex-Cardiff trolleybuses, a former Morris Bros Harrington-bodied coach, former Aberdare UDC NCME-bodied Guy Arab III LNY 854 and a Leyland Tiger Cub. (K. A. Jenkinson)

New to Bristol Omnibus Co. in July 1948, engineless ECW highbridge-bodied Bristol K5G LAE 713 stands in Way's yard at Cardiff Docks alongside former Merthyr Tydfil UDC's Park Royal-bodied Bristol K6A HB 6018, which was new in April 1945. (Author's collection)

One of Cardiff's dual-door, three-axle trolleybuses is being dragged from the storage area to the scrapping bay in Way's yard at Cardiff Docks *c*. 1971. (Author's collection)

Ashes to ashes, dust to dust. Two of the workers in Way's yard at Cardiff Docks, oblivious to environmental concerns, stand and watch the flames devour what is thought to be a former Aberdare UDC double-decker. (Author's collection)

Seen in the yard of AJT Recycling, Fforestfach, in September 2024 are two of First Cymru's Alexander-bodied Volvo B10BLEs driver trainers, W591 RFS and W603 RFS, both of which started life with First Glasgow. (Author's collection)

Ex-Stagecoach South Wales Northern Counties Paladin-bodied Volvo B10M 20870 (P870 MNE), which began life with Stagecoach Manchester in March 1997, is seen here laid on its side at Abba Scrap Metal's Dowlais premises to allow the easy removal of its mechanical units. (Abba Scrap Metal)

Having been cut down by Colbro, Rothwell, for use as a scrap carrier, former West Yorkshire 1938 ECW-bodied Bristol L5G CWT 858 is seen here in 1956 at the company's Jaw Bones works yard where it continued in its new role until being scrapped there during the following year. On the right is another ex-West Yorkshire Bristol L5G awaiting its fate. (T. M. Leach collection)

Awaiting the removal of their electrical equipment, which was then sold to overseas customers, are ex-Newcastle Corporation Sunbeam trolleybuses LTN 481, 506, 514, 507 and 484. They are seen at Colbro's Jaw Bone Works, Rothwell's premises in August 1965. (K. A. Jenkinson)

Scattered across the Stratford-upon-Avon quarry of dealers/breakers Bird's in the early 1960s are numerous ex-London Transport RTs and ex-Birmingham Corporation Daimlers, together with a few buses from independent operators. (Author's collection)

Awaiting scrapping in the deep mud at the foot of Bird's Stratford-upon-Avon quarry early in 1965 are ex-Birmingham Corporation Metro Cammell-bodied Daimler CVD6s HOV 759, 790 and 801 and former London Transport Park Royal-bodied RT KGK 720, which still looked reasonably complete at that time. (F. W. York collection)

Although dominated by former Birmingham Corporation buses, a trio of ex-London Transport RTs (one of which is on its side) can also be spied in this view of Bird's Stratford-upon-Avon quarry in the early 1960s. (F. W. York collection)

This long-distance view of Bird's quarry at Stratford-upon-Avon in 1965 shows a selection of the vehicles awaiting destruction and highlights the size and depth of the area. (F. W. York collection)

With its mechanical units already removed, former West Midlands Special Needs Transport's Mercedes-Benz L609D minibus M693 ROM, which was new in June 1995, forlornly awaits its fate at Lloyd's, Hixon, in October 2022. (Paul Emery)

Being scrapped in the yard of UK Bus Dismantlers at Bromyard is this unidentified Leyland Lynx. (Author's collection/Clive Noble)

Seen partly dismantled in the Spondon yard of breakers Looms in 2022 is a former Notts & Derby (Wellglade) Plaxton-bodied Volvo B7TL. (Author's collection/Daniel Harrison)

Nearing their end in Looms' Spondon's yard in September 2022 are, from left to right: Trent Barton (Wellglade) Wright-bodied Scania L94UBs FJ03 VVX and FJ03 VWM and Volvo B7RLE FJ58 KJV. (Author's collection/Chris Gaskin)

The rear section of ex-First Bus 10186 and an unidentified example are seen loaded onto a trailer in Blakeleys' Platt Bridge yard in 2021. (Author's collection)

Ex-First Bus Wright-bodied Scania L94UB T579 JNG and Volvo B6BLE W825 PFB stand alongside former Ebley Coaches Alexander (Belfast)-bodied Volvo Olympian N430 FKK, which began life with Dublin Bus registered 96-D-277, in the abandoned yard of breaker Blakeleys at Platt Bridge in 2022. (K. A. Jenkinson)

An unidentified Mercedes-Benz minibus is seen here sandwiched between former First Bus Plaxton-bodied Dennis Dart SLF R422 WPX and an ex-Darwen Coach Services Stagecoach-liveried Alexander-bodied (Belfast) Mercedes Bens 709 in the abandoned Platt Bridge yard of Blakeleys in 2021. (K. A. Jenkinson)

Resting in the yard of Booth's, Rotherham, after being converted to a scrap carrier, is former Greater Manchester Transport Metro Cammell Orion-bodied Leyland PD2/40 UNB 549, behind which is hiding a similarly converted ex-South Yorkshire PTE AEC Regent V. (Author's collection/Adrian Griffith)

Two ex-London Transport Green Line RFs and country area RF625 stand with a former Alexander Northern Leyland PD2 double-decker in the Rotherham yard of Booth's in 1975. (B. Newsome collection)

Standing alongside a railway carriage in the Rotherham yard of breakers Booth's in November 1980 are ex-South Yorkshire PTE Leyland PDR1/2 LWB 126D and AEC Swift TWE 121F, both of which carry Park Royal bodywork. (Author's collection/ Adrian Griffith)

With only a few more days of its life remaining, ex-West Riding Roe-bodied Leyland PS2/12A EHL 345 is pictured here in Dunscroft Commercial's yard in May 1974. (Leo Pratt)

Roe-bodied Leyland Atlantean AN68 1762 (CWG 762V), which was new to South Yorkshire PTE in 1979, was repainted into the livery of Premier Coaches, Stainforth (who it had taken over in 1988), in order to promote Premier's bus and coach hire business. Here it is seen being stripped in the Yard of Jameson (Doncaster Bus Breakers) in November 1992. (B. Newsome collection)

One of Leeds City Transport's ex-London Feltham trams, purchased from the capital in 1950, is seen here being scrapped in Leeds by breaker George Cohen in 1959. (Author's collection)

This unfortunately poor-quality photograph illustrates Paul Sykes' original site at Blacker Hill Sidings, Barnsley, in the late 1960s. (Author's collection)

Seen at Joe Sykes' Blacker Hill Sidings yard, Barnsley, on 2 October 1979 is ex-Greater Glasgow PTE Alexander-bodied Leyland PRD1/1 Atlantean LA315 (GYS 891D), which was new in August 1966. (Adrian Griffith)

A pair of former East Yorkshire Motor Services Willowbrook-bodied AEC Regent Vs await their fate at an unidentified breaker's site at Blacker Hill Sidings, Barnsley, in 1971. (John Law)

Paul Sykes moved from Blacker Hill Sidings, Barnsley, to a new site at Shaw Lane, Carlton. It is at the latter where several buses and coaches are seen here being dismantled by him in the late 1970s. (Author's collection)

Seen standing alone at Whiting Bros' Featherstone site in July 1970 is ECW-bodied Bristol K6B KNG 375, which began life with Eastern Counties in December 1969. (Leo Pratt)

Seen in February 1963 partly dismantled in the snow at Dennis Higgs' premises at Monk Bretton is former Keighley West Yorkshire ECW lowbridge-bodied Bristol K6B KDB13 (FWX 834), which was new in March 1948 and, as can be seen, had retrospectively been fitted with staggered double seats on the upper deck. (K. A. Jenkinson)

Still complete but next in line for scrapping, ex-Castlepoint Bus Co. former Bristol Omnibus ECW lowbridge-bodied Bristol KSW6B OHY 935 and Confidence, Leicester, UOO 500, a Bristol LD6B new to Southern National in 1957, stand in the yard of Carlton Metals in the autumn of 1979. (Jeremy Dickinson)

New to Standerwick, Blackpool, in October 1971 and ending its operational life with Hulme Hall School, Cheadle Hulme, ECW-bodied Bristol VRL OCK 67K stands alongside a Wilts & Dorset ex-London Transport MCCW-bodied Fleetline at PVS, Carlton, in 1991 with various other buses including some ex-Clydeside Routemasters forming the backdrop. (Jeremy Dickinson)

A 1991 view of PVS's yard from the adjacent disused railway embankment shows a variety of buses and coaches, including a trio of ex-Lincolnshire Road Car Bristol VRTs and, closest to the camera, former London Buses RM1323. (Jeremy Dickinson)

Facing the lens in the extremely muddy yard of PVS at Carlton in February 1991 are ex-London Transport Park Royal-bodied Leyland B20 Fleetlines OJD 404R and THX 475S with other buses of this type, Leyland Nationals, an AEC Swift and a Bristol VRT in the background. (Jeremy Dickinson)

Piled in a heap in Ripley's Carlton yard in 1992 are three ex-National Welsh Leyland Nationals. The one on the ground facing forward is N572. (Jeremy Dickinson)

PVS's tightly packed yard in the 1990s featuring buses of various types, already with their engines removed, quietly waiting their turn to move into the scrapping area. (Jeremy Dickinson)

Seen in PVS's yard in 1992 alongside an ex-Midland Red Leyland National is the front section of a former Dutch (Centraal, Rotterdam) bendibus purchased from dealer W. North, Sherburn-in-Elmet, upon its closure in January 1991. (Jeremy Dickinson)

Lined up awaiting scrapping at Joe Sykes' yard, Carlton, in August 1980 are a Bristol FS6G and a number of ex-Midland Red single-deckers, with S21 type 5874 nearest the camera. (Jeremy Dickinson)

Being dismantled by hand in Joe Sykes' Carlton yard in 1980 is ex-Eastbourne Corporation 49 (DHC 649), an East Lancs-bodied AEC Regent V which was new in March 1956. (Jeremy Dickinson)

New to West Yorkshire PTE's Halifax division, this low-height Northern Counties-bodied Daimler Fleetline, which spent most of its working life at Todmorden depot, is seen here being dismantled by Joe Sykes, Carlton, in August 1980. (Jeremy Dickinson)

Huddled together in Dave Rollinson's Carlton yard in the January 1985 snow are ex-London Transport Routemaster RMs ALD 920B and ALD 875B together with ex-London RMC CUV 231C. (Jeremy Dickinson)

Partly dismantled and standing in Meynell's Boulder Bridge Lane yard, Carlton, are ex-Greater Manchester Transport MCW-bodied Daimler CRG6 Fleetlines PNA 242J, PNA 210J, and an unidentified example. (K. A. Jenkinson)

Former Crosville Bristol FS6B JFM 212D stands in the yard of Goodwin, Carlton, in front of ex-Hants & Dorset Bristol FS6Bs 7675 LJ and 4697 RU, all of which had arrived from dealer Martins of Middlewich in May 1979. (Jeremy Dickinson)

New to PMT in July 1969 and having served the company for a mere ten years, Marshall-bodied Daimler SRP8 Roadliner WEH 137G is seen here in Tommy Goodwin's yard, Carlton, in October 1979. (Jeremy Dickinson)

Laid on its side in the yard of Tom Goodwin, Carlton, in the early 1990s is a former South Wales Transport Leyland National. Waiting their fate in the background are six ex-Merseybus Leyland Atlanteans. (Jeremy Dickinson)

Three ex-Merseybus Alexander-bodied Leyland AN68A/1R Atlanteans – HTJ 640P (left), GKA 471L (centre) and GKA 512M (right) – are seen here being dismantled by Goodwin at Carlton in November 1994. (Jeremy Dickinson)

Barnsley breaker Ken Askin's Foden wagon is seen here suspended-towing an ex-Maidstone & District single-decker, which is itself towing one of its sisters en route to his Barnsley yard. (Author's collection/Mike Rhodes)

Although former Lancashire United Transport Marshall-bodied Leyland PSUC1/11 Tiger Cub 242 (ETJ 125F) is already well on its way to its total destruction at Parton & Allen's Carlton Yard in 1981, it surprisingly still retains its destination blinds. (Jeremy Dickinson)

Sporting severe roof damage and seen here in the yard of M&S Parton on 23 June 2022 is East Lancs-bodied Volvo Olympian R357 XVX, which was new to Harris Bus, West Thurrock, in August 1997 but had ended its days in non-PSV use. (K. A. Jenkinson)

Bordering each other's premises at Shaw Lane/Boulder Bridge Lane, Carlton, the three buses facing forward are in Hardwick's yard while all the others behind are awaiting their fate in PVS's premises. (Author's collection)

Lined up in Hardwick's Carlton yard in July 2011 are a handful of ex-Stagecoach Alexander-bodied MAN single-deckers and a double-decker formerly in the fleet of Arthurs Coaches, Airdrie. (Paul Emery)

Pictured here at breaker Alan Hardwick's Carlton site on 23 June 2022 are ex-Stagecoach West Optare Solo VX07 LXZ, former Stagecoach East Midlands Transbus SLF YN04 YXX and Alexander-bodied MAN 14.280 FX08 HFB. (K. A. Jenkinson)

Seen being pushed into line by a mechanical bucket in PVS's Carlton yard is a former South Wales Transport ECW-bodied Bristol VRT, whose engine and rear wheels have been removed. (K. A. Jenkinson)

Former SUT Sheffield Leyland National UCO 47L, which was new to Plymouth City Transport in May 1973, is seen here alongside two former Lothian Alexander-bodied Leyland Atlanteans (the centre one being OSF 947M) in Wigley of Carlton's yard in early 1991. (Jeremy Dickinson)

Also seen in Wigley's premises in August 1991 with its windows smashed and its rear axle and engine removed is former Western National ECW-bodied Bristol VRT BFJ 168L. (Jeremy Dickinson)

It is not unusual to see buses stacked on top of each other in Wigley's cramped Carlton yard, as illustrated by this ex-Stagecoach Optare Solo on top of another single-decker on 15 March 2017. In the foreground are the remains of a First Group vehicle's chassis. (K. A. Jenkinson)

Former Wright, Wrexham, ex-Greater Manchester Transport Leyland Titan ANE 4T is seen here after having its engine removed in the snow in Wigley's Carlton yard in the 1990s. (Jeremy Dickinson)

Looking down into Ripley's Carlton yard from the adjacent railway line in January 1991 a wide array of different vehicle models from numerous different operators can be seen, as can hordes of scrap metal in the left foreground. (Jeremy Dickinson)

Spending its last hours in PVS's Carlton yard at the start of February 1991, former Camms of Nottingham's ex-Kingston-upon-Hull Corporation Scania Metropolitan KRH 417P enjoys its final hours. (Jeremy Dickinson)

Lined up in the rear yard of Ripley, Carlton, in 1995 are a selection of buses being used for spares. The Leyland National in the middle is FTN 704W, while on the left is an ex-Leon Finningley former Great Manchester double-decker. (Jeremy Dickinson)

Geoff Ripley was a major purchaser of Rossendale Transport's time-expired buses for several years, one of which was this Handyrider-branded unidentified MCW Metrorider, seen well on its way towards oblivion in 1999. (Author's collection)

A trio of Mass Transit, North Anston, former London Buses Leyland Titans, including KYN 310X, stand with other double-deckers in the Carlton premises of breaker Geoff Ripley in early 2009. (B. Newsome collection)

It's hard to believe that this was once a Roe-bodied Leyland Atlantean AN68 double-decker. Starting life with London Country in May 1981 and latterly a promo bus for *Jobs & Training Weekly* magazine, KPJ 284W is seen here dismantled and crushed in Ripley's Carlton yard in 2008. (Paul Emery)

Having only a few days earlier arrived in Ripley's Carlton yard, seen on 19 October 2023 is Stagecoach Selkent accident-damaged ADL EnviroE400Hmmc-bodied Alexander Dennis E40H 12372 (YX16 OGL). (Paul Emery)

The lower deck of English Electric-bodied Leyland TD3 AFY 973, which was new to Southport Corporation in November 1934, stood guard at the entrance to Wombwell Diesels' premises for several years in the 1970s. (B. Newsome collection)

This unfortunately poor-quality photograph (included for its historic value) provides a panoramic view of Wombwell Diesels' yard in the mid-1980s. It is surprisingly devoid of ex-London RTs, which dominated the site for several years. (Jeremy Dickinson)

Ten ex-London Transport Metro Cammell-bodied AEC Regal IV RFs (including nearest camera RF685, RF387 and RF448) stand in line at Wombwell Diesels in 1983 awaiting their ultimate fate. (Jeremy Dickinson)

Ex-London Transport RT 3254 (LLU 613) stands with two of its sisters in the yard of Wombwell Diesels in 1979. Blessed with good fortune, RT 3254 avoided the dreaded torch by being purchased for preservation. (B. Newsome collection)

With almost all of its top deck removed and a large hole cut in its side for use in a TV production, former London Transport RT2946 (MLL 712) is seen here at Wombwell Diesels' premises in 1978 before being completely scrapped. (B. Newsome collection)

Having just arrived at Wombwell Diesels in July 1990, former London Transport Routemasters RMA4, RM1261 and RM1830 have yet to be moved to the scrapping area where they will receive their ultimate fate. (D. Bentley collection)

Wombwell Diesels contributed to global warming in August 1981 when it applied its then usual method of disposing of the remains of a bus which it had stripped of all its resaleable mechanical units and panels, etc. (Jeremy Dickinson)

Seen in the Ferrybridge yard of Whiting Bros on 5 March 1999 – four weeks before its closure – are ex-Village Group, Garston, Alexander-bodied Leyland Fleetline ASD 29T, which had started life with A1 Service (McKinnon), Kilmarnock, in April 1979 and an unidentified ECW-bodied Bristol VRT. (K. A. Jenkinson)

Former Merseybus Alexander-bodied Leyland Atlantean 1939 (ACM 739X), the front axle of which has already been removed, stands alongside ex-Kentishbus PMT-bodied Freight Rover Sherpa D179 CRE in the Ferrybridge yard of breakers Whiting Bros in March 1999. (K. A. Jenkinson)

Standing close to the public highway on an unfenced area alongside Whiting Bros' Ferrybridge yard in April 1993 and flouting environmental regulations are several partly dismantled buses, including an ex-Clydeside Scottish Bristol FLF driver trainer. (K. A. Jenkinson)

Samuel Ledgard's solid-tyred 1914 Karrier U 2706 spent twenty-five years stored on the roof of its owner's Armley depot before being removed to Butler's Bradford yard, where it is seen a few weeks prior to being scrapped in 1952. (J. S. Cockshott)

Being scrapped in Butler's Eller Ghyll yard at Menston in 1953 is ex-Ledgard Bedford OWB JUA 989 and the company's Otley depot towing bus, Leyland PLSC3 KW 4581. (R. F. Mack)

New to Leeds City Transport as a double-decker, all-Crossley DD42 MNW 702 is seen here in Blamires' Bradford yard between two ex-Kingston-upon-Hull Corporation Guy Arabs after being cut down to become a scrap carrier. (B. Newsome collection)

The second prototype ECW-bodied Bristol Lodekka JWT 712, which was new in March 1950, toured the country as a demonstrator before spending all its working life with West Yorkshire Road Car Co. Sadly it was not preserved after its withdrawal from service and is pictured here awaiting its demise in breaker Blamires' Bradford yard. (T. M. Leach collection)

One of six Plaxton-bodied Foden PVSC6 coaches bought new by independent Samuel Ledgard, Leeds, in 1949, MUA 865 is seen here awaiting scrapping in Blamires' Bradford yard soon after its operational days had come to an end in 1967. (T. M. Leach collection)

Standing on a small patch of dry land in 1983 at the foot of Bingley Autospares' waterlogged quarry, where it dumped most of its purchases, are a selection of buses that had started life with Leeds City Transport and Bradford and Halifax Corporations. (B. Newsome collection)

With a former military vehicle standing on its roof, a 1956 ex-Huddersfield Joint Omnibus Committee Roe-bodied AEC Reliance, ECX 887C, rebuilt in 1965 by Hanson, Huddersfield, from 1956 AEC Reliance KVH 363, has already had its interior stripped out here at Bingley Autospares. (B. Newsome collection)

Five ex-West Yorkshire PTE Leyland PD3 double-deckers which had started life with Leeds City Transport are seen here at Bingley Autospares in 1983. (Jeremy Dickinson)

New to Leeds City Transport and Halifax Joint Omnibus Committee respectively, both of which were then swallowed up by West Yorkshire PTE, Leeds, Weymann-bodied Leyland PD3A/2 320 DUA stands alongside Halifax Metro Cammell-bodied Leyland PD3/4 KCP 10 at Bingley Autospares in May 1983. (Jeremy Dickinson)

Seen here being scrapped at an unidentified site are two ex-West Riding's short-lived Guy Wulfrunians. (John Law)

Pictured in S. Motor Spares yard on Grange Mill Lane, Sheffield, in February 2024 are seven unidentified coaches. (Author's collection)

Ex-Yorkshire Rider Northern Counties-bodied Fleetline 7004, former Merseybus Alexander-bodied Atlantean 1366 and ex-Eastern Counties Leyland National PVF 372R are seen here at PVS, Carlton, in 1992. (Jeremy Dickinson)

An unusual find in the Carlton yard of PVS in December 1992 were a pair of Duple-bodied Bedford OBs. The coach on the left – ERG 164 – was sold for preservation while that on the right – FBU 493 – was sold as a source of spares. (Jeremy Dickinson)

After being separated, the front and rear sections of some First Leeds Wright-bodied Volvo B10LA bendibuses are seen awaiting their final scrapping here in PVS's Carlton yard on 22 July 2013. (K. A. Jenkinson)

New to First Northampton in June 1997, Alexander (Belfast)-bodied gas-powered Volvo B10L 66001 (P501 MVV) awaits its fate at PVS's Carlton premises on 28 February 2008. (K. A. Jenkinson)

Seen in the yard of PVS on 15 March 2017 are three roofs removed from the heavily cannibalised ex-London Routemasters standing alongside. Awaiting their transportation to Edinburgh, six roofs had been purchased by Lothian Buses for possible transplanting onto some of their open-top sightseeing RMs. (K. A. Jenkinson)

The first hydrogen buses to appear at Carlton were two tri-axle Van Hool A330s new in 2014 and operated by Stagecoach Bluebird (SV14DMX) and First Aberdeen (SV14 FZD) on behalf of Aberdeen City Council. Here they are seen in PVS's yard on 23 June 2022 after having had their roof-mounted hydrogen tanks removed. (K. A. Jenkinson)

Lined up in the Carlton yard of PVS on 23 June 2022 are a former West Yorkshire Metro BMC FE1100 yellow school bus, two unidentified double-deckers and a former M-Travel Castleford Optare/Irisbus-bodied Irisbus Agora Line, which was the subject of a preservation bid. (K. A. Jenkinson)

Former Plymouth Citybus Plaxton-bodied Volvo B7TL X504 EGK, which was new to Go-Ahead London General, ex-Notts & Derby's former Lothian Alexander-bodied Volvo Olympian N407 GSX and an unidentified coach are seen here with the remains of other PSVs towering skywards in Wigley's Carlton yard in June 2022. (K. A. Jenkinson)

New to Ulsterbus, Wright-bodied Leyland Tiger WXI 4420 stands alongside ex-Vale Travel Optare Solo X312 CBT and an unidentified Wright-bodied bus in Geoff Ripley's yard at Carlton on 2 January 2019. (K. A. Jenkinson)

New to Tyne & Wear PTE in August 1975, Duple-bodied Leyland Leopard PSU3C/4R GBB 994N is seen here in North East Bus Breakers' Annfield Plain yard devoid of all its glass, its interior and most of its panels. (B. Newsome collection)

Tucked between three bread van-type minibuses in the yard of North East Bus Breakers in 1992 is ex-Go-Ahead Northern Leyland National APT 161S. (B. Newsome collection)

Seen here in various stages of demolition at North East Bus Breakers, Annfield Plain, in early 1998 are a trio of ex-Northumbria Leyland Leopard coaches, that on the right being Plaxton-bodied SUP 727V. (B. Newsome collection)

Four ex-Go-Ahead Northern double-deckers are pictured here together with a former Target Travel coach in the Annfield Plain yard of North East Bus Breakers. (B. Newsome collection).

The skeletal remains of four double-deckers previously operated by Bedlington & District – two of which are ex-City of Oxford AEC Regent IIIs – stand in the Ashington yard of breaker Willoughby. (Author's collection)

Fitted with a new 8-foot-wide body on the lengthened early post-war Bristol L5G chassis of GHN 991 in May 1957 for operation on United's Scarborough's seafront service, 996 CHN later passed to Service Coaches, Bebside, before ending its days in breakers Hancock & Turner's Ashington yard where it is seen here *c.* 1972. (Author's collection)

New to United in May 1953, ECW-bodied Leyland PSU1/15 RHN 772 ended its days operating for Bebside Independent Service Coaches before meeting its end here in the Ashington yard of Hancock & Turner in early 1975. (Leo Pratt)

Still complete and pictured here in the Hexham yard of dealer/breaker Ted Heslop in 1974 is all-Leyland TS3 CK 4447, which was new to Ribble in March 1931 and had latterly served as a caravan. (K. A. Jenkinson)

Two layers of buses, totalling eighteen, the majority of which are ex-First Group vehicles, are seen here awaiting scrapping at Alpha Recovery's premises at Weetslade in 2014. (Author's collection)

Dominating this photograph of a variety of buses awaiting their fate at Alpha Recovery's yard at Weetslade is LK53 FAL, an ex-First London Mercedes-Benz 0530G bendibus. (Author's collection)

Looking down the Weetslade yard of Alpha Recovery, buses and coaches from a variety of operators can be seen, some of which are piled on top of each other. (Author's collection)

Both having been part of the Arriva Northumbria fleet, Alexander Dennis Trident NK57 GXF stands alongside Plaxton-bodied Dennis Dart SLF LK53 FAL in a corner of Alpha Recovery's Weetslade yard during their scrapping process on 18 March 2021. (Author's collection)

Having been removed from its 1939 Bristol K5G chassis, which was being overhauled in preparation to being fitted with a new ECW body, the original body of York West Yorkshire YDG 72, seen here in 1955, was being scrapped behind West Yorkshire's Harrogate depot by breaker Kindon from nearby Starbeck, whose wagon is seen behind it. (Bill Counter)

Awaiting their fate in Locke's yard in Edinburgh in July 1968 are ex-SMT Leyland PD2 BB 51 and AEC Regent III HH24 (FFS 172). (John Sinclair)

Standing in the yard of Riccarton (Kilmarnock) breaker Lundie in August 1964 is the old Leyland body from Western SMT Leyland TD4 CS 4506, which was given a new Northern Counties body in 1949. Behind it is the Alexander body removed from Alexander Leyland LT5A WG 3251. (John Sinclair)

Sharing breaker Muir's scrapyard in Kirkcaldy with some Burlingham-bodied Leyland Cheetahs in April 1964 is Roe lowbridge-bodied Guy Arab II AMS 187, which was new to Alexander in September 1944. (John Sinclair)

Decomposing in breaker Kelbie's Turriff quarry in February 1967 after being withdrawn from service two years earlier are the remains of Wemyss of Ardersier's 1948 Leyland PD1A CST 256 (its body built by Samlesbury Engineering to Leyland design) and an unidentified double-decker. (John Sinclair)

Standing in the muddy Terriff yard of breaker Kelbie in 1966 are four partly scrapped Duple-bodied Guy Arab IIIs including AMS 549, which, like the others, was supplied new to Lawsons at Kirkintilloch in 1947. (Campbell Morrison collection)

Protecting the fence surrounding Dunsmore's Larkhall yard is a partly scrapped ex-Kelvin Scottish AEC Routemaster and an unidentified, red-liveried Alexander-bodied double-decker together with an ECW-bodied bus. (Campbell Morrison collection)

Becoming beyond rescuing for preservation are a trio of ex-Eastern Scottish ECW-bodied Daimler Fleetlines stored at one of breaker Dunsmore's Larkhall overspill yards, this one being at West Calder in October 2003. (K. A. Jenkinson)

A wide selection of makes and models of buses and coaches awaiting their ultimate demise are pictured here at Dunsmore's Larkhall, West Calder, overspill site situated alongside operator Prentice Westwood's depot in the 2000s. (Campbell Morrison collection)

Seen in Dunsmore's main yard at Larkhall where most of the dismantling took place is ex-Stagecoach Fife Leyland Titan 742, former Midland Bluebird Leyland Tiger 130 and former Stagecoach Western Leyland National 2 792 (KRS 540V). (Campbell Morrison collection)

Seen here in the Leith yard of breaker Hunter in October 1966 is all-Leyland Tiger TS2 FG 7765, which began life with W. Alexander & Sons but was later used as a caravan. (John Sinclair)

Although largely a dealer, Millburn Motors of Glasgow and Preston also scrapped a number of buses to provide spares for others. Seen here in October 1965 are the remains of W. Alexander's 1935-vintage Leyland TS7 WG 3457, which had begun life as a single-decker but was given this new Alexander lowbridge double-deck body in 1943. (John Sinclair)

Having just arrived at Campbell's yard in August 2024 is an ex-McColls, Dumbarton, Wright Gemini-bodied Volvo B7TL, which had started life with Arriva London North in 2002. (Author's collection/Aaron Love)

Being slowly crushed by cars in the yard of Manx Metals, Ballasalla, Isle of Man, in July 1979 are Park Royal-bodied AEC Regal IV NMN 355 (originally demonstrator WMK 271) and Northern Counties-bodied AEC Regent III KMN 836, both of which had been operated by Douglas Corporation. (K. A. Jenkinson)

Seen laying on its side in the quarry at Point of Ayre used by Manx metal recyclers Motor Salvage in April 1984 is ex-Isle of Man Transport's Weymann-bodied Leyland PD3A/1 LMN 81, which started life with Bournemouth Corporation registered 6160 RU. (K. A. Jenkinson)

Partly scrapped ex-Citybus Alexander-bodied (Belfast) Bristol RELL6G 2479 (WO I8479) enjoys the sunshine as it rests on the grass in breaker Beattie's Hillsborough premises in April 2001. (K. A. Jenkinson)

Burned out by terrorists at a road block on 30 August 1988, Ulsterbus ex-West Yorkshire ECW-bodied Bristol RELL TWX 197L awaits collection by a local scrap dealer in Derry depot's yard while reusable mechanical units are being removed. (K. A. Jenkinson)

Double- and single-deckers lay on their sides in the Ahoghill (Ballymena) premises of metal merchants Thomas Hamill & Sons. While the majority seen here are ex-Ulsterbus vehicles, the single-decker on the top (right) with the yellow front (KLZ 7275) is a former Southern Education and Libraries Board bus. (Author's collection)

Only thirteen years old, after operation by Diamond ex-Transport for Greater Manchester-owned Optare SoloSR diesel-electric hybrid YJ60 KCF awaits its fate in the Carlton yard of breaker PVS in May 2023. (Author's collection/Tony Hunter)

Claimed to be the first 100 per cent electric double-decker in the world when it was retrofitted with a battery-powered electric motor in place of its diesel engine in 2014, Transdev Blazefield City Sightseeing-liveried East Lancs open-top-bodied Dennis Trident T409 SMV looks uncertain about its future as is stands in PVS's Carlton yard on 23 June 2022. (K. A. Jenkinson)

Gas, hybrid and electric buses are now starting to appear regularly in breakers yards, as demonstrated by ex-Reading Buses Alexander Dennis Enviro400 hybrid-powered Trident SN60 EDF, awaiting dismantling at PVS, Carlton, in June 2023. (K. A. Jenkinson)

Two for the price of one. Seen at Transdev Blazefield's Blackburn depot on 6 June 2024 are Team Pennine's Optare Solo's MX08 DHP, sitting on PVS Carlton's four-axle lorry and YK08 ERY being suspended and towed behind it. (Author's collection/ Steven Buckley)

Both buses and railway rolling stock were dismantled side-by-side in the same yard of Booth, Rotherham, as seen with two former London Routemasters keeping company with a couple of railway locomotives on 21 January 1984. (Author's collection)